Ozana Giusca

Business Unlimited
Smarter Profits Faster

- Volume 2 -

Grow Your Sales

101 Zero-Cost Tactics to Take Your Company to the Next Level

Amaze Yourself With What YOU Can Achieve Further!

Copyright © 2017 Ozana Giusca
All rights reserved.

ISBN-13: 978-1978361843
ISBN-10: 197836184X

To all the business owners and entrepreneurs I have worked with: thank you for entrusting me with growing your business.

To my team, who have put so much effort into building Tooliers, the high-end business growth tools and programs that are transforming businesses around the world, a big thank you for going through the ups and downs with me.

Thank you for helping me with this book. We wouldn't be here without your dedication and contribution!

I would like to name the Tooliers core team: Vali, Dragos, Sorana & Catalina. You are like family to me! I am so grateful you joined me in my journey!

Table of Contents

Foreword	V
Preface	VII
My Story	IX
Introduction	1
Bonus • Steady Growth - Systematize Your Business	4
Tactic #1 • Follow a System	5
Note: Tactics #2 - #16 are in Volume 1	
Grow Your Sales	12
Tactic #17 • Use Inducements to Close Sales Now	13
Tactic #18 • Sell More On the Spot	16
Tactic #19 • Turn One of Your Products into 'Attractive Premium'	20
Tactic #20 • Encourage On-the-Spot Purchase via Urgency	23
Tactic #21 • Encourage On-the-Spot Purchase via Better Offer	28
Tactic #22 • Know Your Customers. What Keeps Them Awake at Night?	31
Tactic #23 • Keep Close to Your Customers	34
Tactic #24 • Contact All Customers Soon After Their Purchase	38
Tactic #25 • Develop Partnerships	41
Tactic #26 • Start a Relationship with Your Prospect	46
Tactic #27 • Upgrade to a Sales Machine Organization	50
Tactic #28 • Position Your Product or Service Exclusively	54
Tactic #29 • Follow Your Customer's Needs	58
Tactic #30 • Revisit Your Lists of Past Prospects and Customers	61
Tactic #31 • Sell for Next Year, Not Just for Tomorrow	64
Smart Business System™	68
Bonus • Love Letter	80
Love Letter Template	82
Love Letter Example	83
Glossary of Terms	86

Foreword

The world is changing so fast. These events are opportunities for those who grab them, and at the same time can negatively affect those who do not take action. Most small businesses find it harder to break through their current level. They reach a plateau and do not know what step to take next, or go beyond 'small' and lose the plot.

There is so much information available now about how to run a successful business, but the challenge is to find meaning within this information and to use it appropriately to optimize and grow your business. In my experience as a small business consultant, I have seen a lot of business owners who cannot simply and quickly explain what they do, let alone generate interest and sell their products or services. I also see that entrepreneurs have dreams and goals, yet 80% of their time is spent on things that have no link whatsoever with their objectives. If they do not focus on what is needed to achieve their goals, how can they get there?

If you are looking for a very hands-on approach to building your business from the ground up, Ozana has nailed it in *Business Unlimited*. What a purposeful read for anyone who is an entrepreneur or small business owner. As you continue on your business or career journey, you will face real challenges that may deter you from achieving your biggest goals. The tactics in this book will keep you on track and help you reach your goals in record time.

In our lives we have the opportunity to do it the hard way or to learn from what the experts do, and then do it better. Ozana has been trained by some of the best in the business, including business and marketing guru Jay Abraham. In this new book you will discover key observations and ingredients to create even more success in your life and business. The real-world examples, as well as the practical exercises at the end of each tactic, also ensure this is a user-friendly manual to reaching business success.

Foreword

In *Business Unlimited*, you will learn to see the bigger picture of your business as well as discover the importance of *systematically* improving it; that is, by prioritizing and focusing on those areas that most need improvement. You will learn to identify your best customers; let go of any customers who do not lift your business; learn from your competitors; and fulfil the core purpose of every business: providing *real value* to your customers. You will also discover how creating the right kind of partnerships will grow your business with little extra effort on your part. Business owners will find the tactics on closing sales and creating urgency especially valuable. You will also see how essential it is to build relationships both with your best customers and your team.

This book is also brutally honest about areas in which business owners tend to waste time and resources – and provides a wealth of best practices for time management; this includes a reminder to employ the time-saving advantages of certain technologies. You will also be encouraged to reflect and act upon your role as a leader and to go beyond merely managing your business to making sure it leads to the kind of life and lifestyle you desire. Aspects like personal branding, networking and being open to change are also discussed. Finally, you will clarify your vision in order to take your brand into the future and be left with a business that is dynamic and that constantly strives for – and achieves – improvement and growth.

The bottom line: if you are ready to increase your success rate today, take the time to read this mind-expanding book two to three times, and then implement the ideas that are shared here.

Bill Walsh

America's Small Business Expert

Website: billwalsh360.com

Preface

If you answer YES! to any of these statements, this book is for you.

- You have achieved some success with your business, but seem unable to grow it further.
- You are not satisfied with where your business is.
- You are not getting enough from your business (you are not getting enough recognition or enough money, or you have not succeeded in fully achieving your Objectives).
- Work is taking over your life and you have no time for family, relaxation, or travel.
- You are still struggling to make a living.
- You are bored with your work! You want something more challenging and fun.
- You are missing something, but you're not sure exactly what.
- There are some areas you do not understand (for example, finance) or you are passionate about your product, but you cannot sell it.
- You just want to be sure that you are on top of things and that your business is on the right track.
- You have some ideas for new businesses, but are not quite sure how to go about it.
- You want new challenges, but you need your current business to continue to run for various reasons (financial, community).
- Your turnover and/or profits have started decreasing.
- You can anticipate a disaster but you cannot tell what exactly is happening.
- Your best employees have started to leave.
- You have lost your biggest client.
- You seem to deliver good quality but your clients are still not prepared to pay what you'd like for your products.
- There has been a recent change in your company's industry or outside

Preface

environment and this has had a great impact on your business.
- You and your staff are working too hard and it is just not fair on any of you (especially given the results you achieve).
- You consider your company a victim of your crisis, a system, or something else.
- Your business has stopped serving the community.
- Your business is growing quickly and you are struggling to manage it. It is becoming too complex for you to run on your own.
- Your life is too stressful. There are just too many problems that need to be solved by you, the business owner.
- You and your co-owners have trouble running the business together.
- Your business has started experiencing problems or you foresee problems, but you don't know what to do about them.
- You have accumulated too much debt in your company and can no longer sustain it.
- You simply want to discover the latest strategies that Fortune 500 companies use for their success!

My Story

I want to take a few minutes to ask you the questions that are on every small business owner's mind:

- What is the REAL secret behind businesses that generate more profits while their owners are enjoying life and doing what they want, when they want?
- Can I get more customers to call us instead of *us* chasing *them*?
- How can I get a great team of committed employees to work hard so we grow the business together?
- Is there any way to feel happier with my business and really achieve what I set my mind to?
- Ultimately, how can I, a small business owner, entrepreneur or freelance expert, make a difference in the world?

I get asked these questions all the time and it's why I wrote this book. Via this book, the tools, programs, events we deliver, I provide the answers to these questions, and many more.

Before you dig in, let me tell you a little about myself…

In 2007 my life seemed perfect. I was a rising star, doing everything most people would love to do.

After attaining my MBA from Cass Business School, London in 2000, I worked in the City for a few years. In 2003, I set up my own consulting firm, where I advised on selling a few companies and raised hundreds of millions in bank finance for various projects.

While my business generated a decent income, I knew I was on my way to support other entrepreneurs help more people and make a bigger impact.

With a team of 12 consultants, I was living my dream. I could party, travel, wear my favorite brands…

My Story

I bought a flat, then another one, then an office for our company, a new car... until the financial crisis hit my business badly, as happened with thousands of businesses around the world.

All of a sudden money stopped flowing in. The banks withdrew from financing our transactions; those hundreds of thousands of dollars in success fees never arrived; and ongoing consulting projects got put on hold. No more new business meant no more cash.

Imagine: By January 2009, I had let most of my team go. For me, they were not just staff, they were *family*. And they were damn good at what they did.

With more than a million dollars in debt, I could no longer pay the bank. Many sleepless nights followed... I felt ashamed, convinced people would point a finger at me, accuse me of not paying my debts. I got scared thinking about a potential bad credit rating and that I might never be able to get a loan again.

I felt my reputation as an honest, trustworthy businessperson was ruined as I couldn't pay my debts.

I had no money coming in and was borrowing on a monthly basis to pay my two remaining staff members. I was driving to my father every weekend to get food for the week for me and my partner.

It seemed that every phone call I got, every email I received, brought more bad news.

Watch this: my phone service provider threatening to end my contract should I not pay my bills. Imagine trying to save a business without a phone connection or access to the internet!

That was it, I decided. *Enough!* I borrowed more money and paid for an event in London where 15 successful entrepreneurs shared their strategies on how they became profitable. I learned about online marketing, selling one-to-many via events and social media advertising. Most importantly I realized the need to be visible to the right audience.

How many of these tactics do you think I applied? None! Because I soon realized I was in the wrong business anyway. Yep, this was my biggest take-away from the conference. I realized there was nothing special about me or my business, nothing that would get clients to choose our services.

There were too many people doing the same thing, making it difficult to differentiate myself.

As I had all this cutting edge knowledge, I started applying it to the businesses of former clients, and friends. And *this* is how I started earning again...

It turned out my consulting business was not the only business lacking proper business knowledge! In fact, most small businesses lack such knowledge – they are usually set up based on an opportunity the founder sees, based on the founder's skills and abilities. Yet businesses are complex and no entrepreneur can know it all; certainly no one can handle everything.

I also discovered my special gift: being able to identify where a business is leaving money on the table and how they can double or even triple their profits by making a few important changes.

My skill became immediately obvious as I managed to achieve:

- **30% increase in Sales within a month** for a client in hospitality (hotel) and a **287% increase in their online bookings within three months.** Their occupancy rate was 10% when we started working together – now it's in excess of 50%.

- **8 Sales during the first workshop** for a weight loss solution – a full house event achieved within five days of promotion. In fact, we had to close the doors and leave people outside disappointed.

- **$40,000 in Sales generated for a book** that had been sitting idle on Amazon before

With the right tools YOU too can turn your business around

My Story

we started working with the author/chiropractor.

- **15% increase in Sales** for the main distributor of promotional materials, who already had 50% market share.

Over the past three years, I have personally helped more than 100 companies achieve massive growth. Some companies increased Sales by 30% within the first month of working with us; others tripled their Sales within a year.

I put all the knowledge I gathered – and much more – into what is today known as **Business Lens™**, a toolkit to identify what business owners don't do well or enough of in their company. This is **a tool that reveals the naked truth about any business**. It measures, mathematically, the gap between your company and Best Practices. The bigger the gap, the more growth potential the company has. Plus, it shows business owners where they need to focus to maximize Sales and profits.

This was the start of Tooliers, the platform with Smart Business solutions for small enterprises to increase profitability and become leaders in their niche. We now have clients around the globe and what's most important is not that we are making money, but that we help those who need us and our tools to smarten their businesses and achieve bigger profits faster.

Above all, I am proud of having built something that lasts beyond me. I know people will benefit from my current activities even after I am no longer here.

What's really in it for me? Or you?

> *When you focus on the right things in your business, you have the recipe to success*

FREEDOM!

The freedom to do what I want, when I want; to live anywhere in the world… and most importantly to be ME!

> *So what does this have to do with you and your business?*

You too can have the FREEDOM you want!

And I guess this is one reason you are reading this – you know you can do more and you want to.

The economy changes rapidly these days. As a small business owner, it is easy to run your business as if lost in a dark forest, thinking only of *survival*. You might forget about the destination. You are most likely involved with paying the next bill, dealing with a crisis after your best employee has left, trying to make up for that lost customer, deciding what kind of paper to buy for the copy machine and many other activities that keep you 'busy' and working hard.

But do you work *smart*? What if there was **a better way to achieve those dreams** you had when you started your business?

One third of business owners **want to grow their businesses, but don't know how and where to start**. The rest would like to maintain their business. The reality, however, is that 80% of businesses fail in the first five years and 96% in the first 10 years (this according to Michael Gerber, author of The *E-Myth*).

These facts also inspired me to write this book. I want to help YOU, a business owner, to *enjoy* your entrepreneurship. I want to help driven entrepreneurs just like you to achieve the success you deserve.

Business Unlimited is a collection of Best Practices I have seen and learned during my 20-year career in professional services. I learned about these tactics from seminars, workshops, conferences and summits,

My Story

and I have tried and tested them on my business and on our clients' businesses. When you master the tactics that follow, you will be able to compete with multinational companies, with Fortune 500 companies, as their equal. Because you know what? They use exactly the same tactics you are about to discover.

This book is part of my mission to empower 1,000,000 entrepreneurs to change the world while they achieve their personal and professional objectives fast, with ease.

Happy reading and enjoy the transformation of your business!

Ozana

Your Smarter Profits Accelerator

P.S. If you are serious about growing your Sales and profits, raising your profile and helping way more people, I invite you to join any of my online or live Master Classes and bootcamps.

Visit My Events Page **(www.ozanagiusca.com/my-events)** to get the updated schedule of my events and register to those most suitable for you.

Why have I written this book?

I wrote this book because I believe YOU can achieve much more especially in today's economy, which is the best possible environment for driven entrepreneurs and small businesses to really take off and finally get to the next level, especially because of the Internet and technology developments.

I believe that small businesses are changing the world and making it a better place... provided they deploy the right systems. Thus, this book is about a systematic approach to business so you achieve your dreams and gain the respect you deserve.

Turning around my own company from the brink of bankruptcy in 2008 to a business selling on all continents was an incredible journey. Having been through 3 years with no sales (before Tooliers took off), I made every possible mistake. I also realised that business can be fun. So I made it my mission to empower 1,000,000 entrepreneurs to make a bigger impact, by proving them with full clarity on their business, and, of course, the right tools. Bottom line, I want to reduce the entrepreneurial struggle by encouraging small business owners and experts to first think strategically and then implement any tactic they consider. This way, they finally get results quickly with no stress or overwhelm.

This book is about sharing some of the lessons we've learnt so you build a profitable business and unleash your unlimited potential... **hence BUSINESS UNLIMITED**.

You hear me talk about Smart Business, which is the vehicle to get there... A Smart Business is flexible in approach, leverages what you have and know, and systematically attracts clients online so you scale and grow exponentially. This, of course, enables you, its founder and commander, to be anywhere you want, and not chained to your desk 16 hours per day.

My Story

Regardless of being early stage or a successful entrepreneur, if you are driven to achieve more, to create more value, to serve more people and improve their lives while you get what you want, then I would love to support you in your journey.

Let's change the world together!

Introduction

How to use this book

You don't have to start with Tactic 1, or to read this collection chronologically. Start with the tactic that feels the most interesting to you. Each tactic addresses a different Stage of a business. You may find one tactic more relevant than another. Read the relevant ones first and feel free to jump from one tactic to another.

You will see that each of the 101 Tactics concludes with a short exercise that will make it easy to apply the tactic to your business. If you are serious about growing your business, it is essential that you *decide how to apply* the tactic you have just read and *do the exercises* that follow. While doing the exercises, write down whatever comes to mind.

Don't get overwhelmed by all the information in this book. You don't have to use it all at once. However, you will be surprised by how much of this book applies to you and your business. Take the knowledge on board, and don't get desperate if you can't find a way of using it on the spot. The more you practice using these tactics, the more ideas you will get – in time you may even find ways to use those tactics you thought were not relevant to your business.

Revisit the book as your business Needs and Goals change. Reread certain tactics, or tackle new ones. This book may well become your 'Bible for a Smarter Business'.

Introduction

The finer details

Definitions of all words or terms that appear in ***bold and italics*** or starting with Caps can be found in the Glossary of Terms.

I use **customer** as a generic term. In your industry, you may prefer the word client, visitor, guest, user, or patient, for example.

I use examples from **a range of industries**. Feel free to adapt and apply the tactics to your own business.

Throughout the book, I use **products** and **services** interchangeably. Note, however, that an **offering** is not the same as a product or service. For our purposes, an offering refers to the product or service combined with its price, packaging and positioning. So, product X as offering A is sold for $100 as a stand-alone product. Product X could also be packaged as offering B, which includes another item or addresses a different market or just has a different packaging, and sells for $200.

Example:

> Cashew nuts can be sold in large quantities (tons) to wholesalers, who then repackage the nuts in smaller quantities (say 1 kilogram) to be sold at the market. Those same cashew nuts can be sold in supermarkets in packs of 300 grams; these look more attractive and command a higher price. Or the cashew nuts can be sold per 100 grams in a high-end bar, for a premium price.
>
> The product is the same – cashew nuts – but with different packaging and/or positioning, it becomes a different offering and commands a different price.
>
> The target market could be the same or different. I could be buying a 1 kg pack at the market, but I could also buy the 300 gram packs in gas stations.

Introducing Tooliers®

Tooliers® (www.tooliers.com) is THE latform with high-end business growth solutions to empower entrepreneurs to build their SMART business so they increase profitability, reduce struggle and become leaders in their niche.

Business Lens™ is the digital mirror of your business. It shows you the naked truth about your business. It shows your unrealized growth potential.

Business Lens™ Diagnosis is the process of using Business Lens™ to perform a full analysis of your business, which identifies the areas that need more of your attention so you take your business to the next level.

Business Doctor is one of our growth programs, where we perform the Business Lens™ Diagnosis, and issue suggestions and recommendations for tactics and strategies to execute, so you grow your business immediately as well as long term.

Businesses don't grow unless people grow. You rock! By reading this book, you are enabling personal growth together with business growth!

Bonus:
Steady Growth -
Systematize Your Business

Follow a System

Focus your efforts exactly where they are required as your business grows

I have created the **Business Growth Focus Formula** (see below) because so often I see business owners focusing on the wrong things. You want to do what you like to do, or what you are best at and this is fine to a certain extent. But if you want to have a *highly successful business*, you need to approach it systematically, and change Focus according to which Stage your business is at. Focus doesn't mean you only work on a certain area of your business or that you do it all by yourself. It means you **concentrate your efforts on a particular area of your business at a particular time.** It also means that you learn more about that area. Of course, you can involve Experts and you can Delegate, as long as this area is where your mind is. Even if you outsource, you inevitably acquire more knowledge in that area.

Be disciplined and Focus on what you have to in order to reach your Objectives and fulfill your dreams

The idea is simple: your Focus, as the owner of the business, moves from 'Sales' to 'Sources and Resources' to 'Systems', as your company grows. This is the **best business growth strategy**. Focusing on one part of the business does not mean that you *only* deal with that part. It means, say, that you allocate half of your time to it, while the other half is split between anything else you would normally deal with. Above all, you, as the business owner, must focus on what needs your Focus, even if it is not necessarily what you *like* doing.

Let's talk about each area of a business:

Business Growth Focus Formula

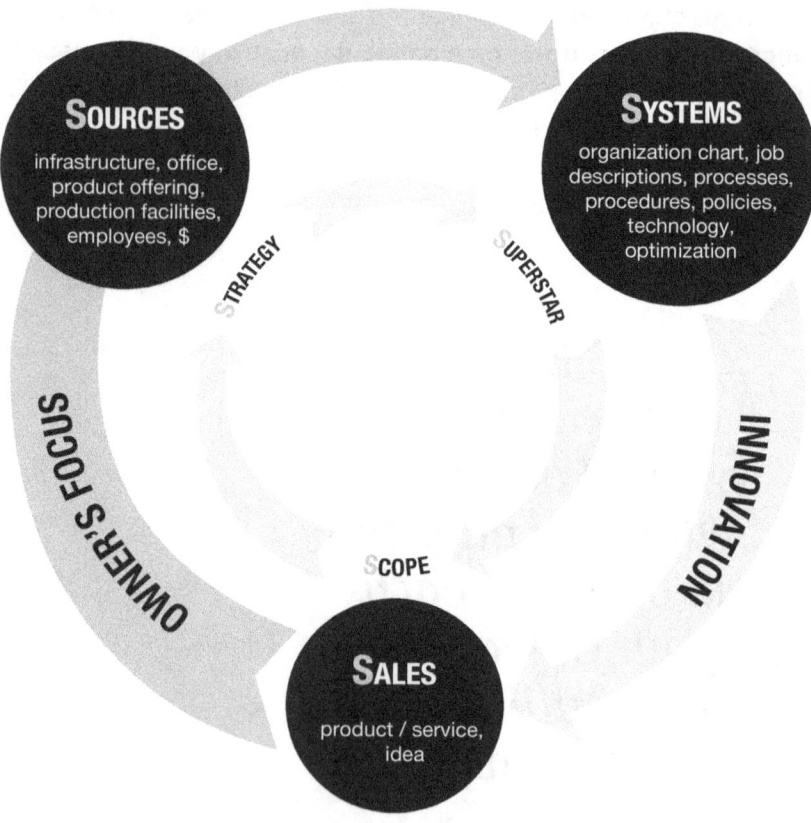

1 Focus on Sales

When you are at the beginning with your business, or when you launch a new product or open a new location. 'Sales' is split into two parts:

(i) selling your product or service;

(ii) selling your idea.

Selling your product or service is what you would generally understand as: giving your product / service to your customer in exchange for money (the price paid).

Selling your idea means getting people to buy into what you are doing. To share your dream, your vision and to get others excited about it. Selling your idea to current employees, potential employees, partners, suppliers, banks and any other person who is necessary to run the business smoothly, is as important as selling your product. You cannot create a business on your own. To achieve your Objectives, you need people around you. And those people don't join just because you think they should. It is tempting to believe they see and understand as you do, but they don't. You have to give them reasons to opt in, just as you give reasons to your customers to buy your product.

During this Stage, you have only a **Scope**. You know where you want to get to, but it is still flexible. You need the market reaction and partners' Feedback in order to ensure you have the right product, the right offering, both for your *customers* and for your business partners. The offering for the *customer* is a widely used concept: 'Buy this product for this price because it solves this problem in this way.' The offer for *business partners* sounds something like this: 'Bring customers to our business and you get x% from all the money they spend with us.' This is how you have to think of the Value proposition for your customers and your business partners. All parties have to win. And everything has to make sense and be clear from the outset.

2. Focus on Sources and Resources

Once your product or service sells by itself; in other words, when customers buy your product or service without you having to convince each of them individually. By 'Sources' I mean everything that enables you to deliver to your customer; that is, your overall infrastructure: production facility, office space, logistics, as well as your employees and money to buy raw materials and invest in further growth. No point selling if you can't deliver, right?

When you have gotten to this phase, **you have a Strategy in place.** Now that you know what and how you sell, and for how much, you can create Specific Objectives and a clear path to achieving them.

3. Focus on System

When you are confident that you have a product that sells and that you can deliver and satisfy your customer. By 'Systems', I mean organizational charts, job descriptions, processes, procedures, policies, IT system, and potentially CRM / ERP (software to help with planning and managing your Resources and your customers).

In this phase you **consolidate what you have**; you organize things internally and clean up your mess. By this Stage, you and your staff have tried various ways of producing and delivering Value and you now know who does what in your company, and how. It is therefore time to document everything that is happening in your company, to put order in place. This helps you and your current employees to better understand how things are being done in your company and to become more efficient. Having these Systems in place also makes for an easier and more efficient process when you bring new people into your organization. You have 'machinery' that works, effectively and efficiently.

What you care about now is **becoming a Superstar Company**. By 'Superstar', I mean being the best in your niche. If you think of your industry as a pyramid, there is only one company on top, a few on the second layer, then the third, and so on... until the bottom, where you find plenty of companies. Your Objective is to **get as close as possible to the top**. Why? Because if anything destructive happens in the economy or in your industry, or if anything happens that can adversely affect your business, you hardly feel it if you are on top. The financial crisis in 2008 resulted in many companies going bankrupt or being close to bankrupt – this is because they were at the bottom of the pyramid in their niche. If a tsunami comes, or the state does construction on the road in front of your shop or office, you need to be in such a strong position that your business does not suffer. This is being a Superstar Company.

After Systems are in place, you need to focus on **Innovation** if you want to take your company to the next level, in which case you go back to Sales in another growth cycle. Alternatively, you retire or sell your company (or you leave it as is and continue to manage 'in the business', which may eventually go downhill).

> *Shift Focus as your company develops and grows*

TAKE ACTION NOW!

Based on the Stage of your business development, decide which of the three areas discussed above requires your Focus. Write it down:

_____
_____
_____
_____
_____

What are your biggest current Challenges? Write these here; then use the tactics in this book to find ways of overcoming these Challenges.

Challenge 1:
_____
_____

Challenge 2:
_____
_____

Challenge 3:
_____
_____

Challenge 4:
_____
_____

Challenge 5:
_____
_____

Grow Your Sales

Use Inducements to Close Sales Now

Make it a no-brainer for your customers to buy NOW

Consider offering something extra in order to close the deal on the spot. Estée Lauder introduced the idea of **Gift with Purchase** and Jay Abraham introduced the idea of **Risk Reversal**, whereby buyers can 'reverse' the transaction if they are not happy; i.e. they return the product to the seller and get their money back. Risk Reversal is about overcoming the client's fear or reluctance to purchase by offering to 'guarantee purchase' and/or to refund without any explanation being required from the client.

By offering that something extra, you increase your closing ratio. You get those *potentials* who are not 100% sure about the purchase to decide on the spot. You also get those people who simply cannot take a decision to buy then and there. People may like your product, they may consider buying it, but this is no guarantee of purchase. This something extra is the 'kick' they need to make the purchase.

Big brands include classic Inducements into their closing process to motivate people to buy faster or with greater enthusiasm, such as:

(i) Buy one; get one free
(ii) Get a second product at half price
(iii) Coupons on purchase
(iv) Points or rewards on purchase
(v) **Gift with Purchase**.

After reading this, you will notice many more examples in your daily life. You don't need to go further than your local supermarket. Use these techniques as inspiration for your own Inducements.

Risk Reversal has been used for a long time by most large stores. Usually you can get a refund for a product within 28 or 30 days. More recently, this Strategy is being used by companies that provide training courses. For example, when I signed up for the Tony Robbins Business Mastery course, I was assured – in writing, on the sign-up form – that if I did not find a million dollar's worth of Value in the course after the first day, I would receive a full refund. The four-day course cost almost half my MBA and this insurance helped me make my decision to buy the course. It minimized my risk. I could also get 25% of the course for free and leave after the first day with a full refund. The course was amazing, so I stayed.

Make it work for you!

> *You don't have to be Tony Robbins to offer insurance and use Risk Reversal. As a nutritionist, you can offer a cash back guarantee on your eating program: if your patient does not lose a certain (minimum) amount of weight within a week of applying your advice, she gets a full refund. If she doesn't lose that weight, you know she is not following your advice and don't want her as your client anyway.*

TAKE ACTION NOW!

Write down 3 ideas for Inducements to close your Sales:

1. _____
   _____
   _____

2. _____
   _____
   _____

3. _____
   _____
   _____

Tactic #18 — Grow Your Sales

Sell More On the Spot

> *A customer who purchases one item from you is in 'Buying Mode'.*
> *Use this window of opportunity to sell more*

Offer your customers other products when they make a purchase, and preferably immediately after they have decided on the purchase. **Make sure you offer relevant products, whether complementary or similar.** When you look for a book on Amazon, you are shown other books purchased by customers who bought that book. Amazon uses this technique because they expect you to buy the book you are looking at, as well as one of the other books shown. Of course the books they show you are relevant to your search!

More Sales per customer of course means overall increased Sales. You have the customer at the ready – making a purchase – so why not encourage them to make another purchase? If you offer an additional product when the customer makes the purchase, they are more likely to buy, because they are in Buying Mode. They feel like buying, so if there is something interesting for them, they will most likely buy that additional item too. Research shows that 80% of people buy additional products on the spot. This is the cheapest way to increase your Sales. Indeed, it doesn't cost you *anything* to offer another product, the client is happy, and you increase bottom line Sales.

They've put it into practice!

> *Recently I popped into an Estée Lauder store to buy day cream. While there, I found a body milk, which I decided to purchase. When I got to the till, the assistant pointed to a stack of boxes next to her with a combo of products and asked if I would like one. 'It's only $15 for you today,' she said. 'It is a great deal, if you consider that the mascara alone costs $10.' What do you*

> *think I did? I was in Buying Mode and it was easy to say yes. If, however, an Estée Lauder rep had come up to me in the street with the same offer, I wouldn't have bought it. If I had received a newsletter from the store offering me the product, I might have considered it. The effect is not as powerful as catching me while in a shopping mood and making it effortless for me to buy on the spot.*

Notice the message the cashier gave me: 'It's only $15 for you today. It is a great deal, if you consider that the mascara alone costs $10.'

Do you think she came up with that message herself? I doubt it. Yes, it's possible, but most likely her manager gave her that message and she learnt it by heart.

The point? Whenever you make an offer, it needs to be presented correctly to the potential client. And if you have sales staff working for you, you need to give them such a message. Now, if you are the one making the sales, you need to have such a message prepared and ready to use.

If you sell online, this tactic is a must. When someone goes towards purchase on your site, ask if they would like to add product X (a Complementary or Similar Product) as well. Research shows that if you do this correctly and appropriately, 80% of customers will add the extra product.

Here is how we do it. Get inspiration from the product journey we've created for our clients, where once they say yes to us, we propose the full solution, which of course consists of more products. Because hey, business today is complex, and entrepreneurs need to have the full, comprehensive picture. This is why the Ozana's Inner Circle™ became so popular with small business owners who want to achieve their objectives faster. They invest initially in one of our products, they get value, and many decide on the spot to continue their business growth journey with us and invest in the entire solution.

Grow Your Sales

Others simply invest in the next product which I suggest to them - it is all thought out in advance though. I have developed a Product Journey, where I know what to suggest next, when someone invests in one of our products.

Design a Product Journey for your customer

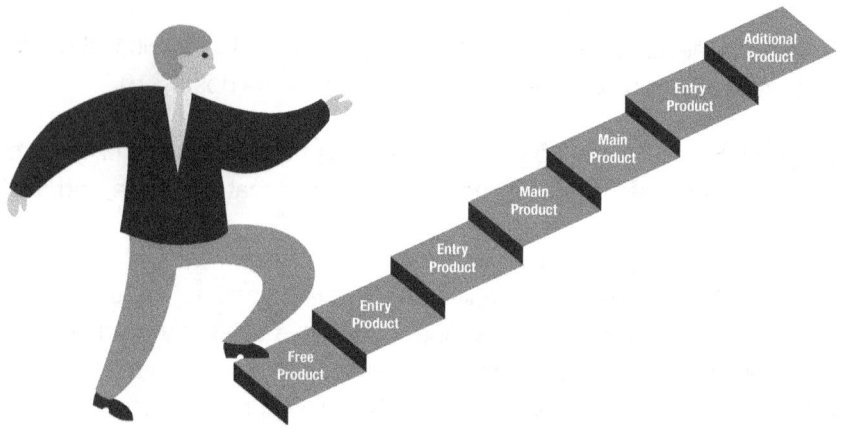

TAKE ACTION NOW!

Write down 3 products you could offer when your customers make a purchase. These should be products that can be added to the shopping cart immediately.

1. _____
   _____
   _____

2. _____
   _____
   _____

3. _____
   _____
   _____

Tactic #19

Turn One of Your Products into 'Attractive Premium'

> Become the toy in the
> McDonalds Happy Meal box

Something is an **Attractive Premium** if people would be happy to receive it when purchasing something else; i.e. when the product is of interest to the customers of a different product. **When your product is an Attractive Premium you don't have to sell it yourself.** It is sold by the partnering business that uses your product to sell more of their product(s).

The McDonalds Happy Meal has been a big hit for more than three decades. A simple yet effective technique sustained this success: the toy included in the food box made this menu choice irresistible to kids. It might be less straightforward for your product, but you can nevertheless find your own product that is the 'toy in the food box'.

Choose one product (to start with) to be used as Attractive Premium by another business. If you sell key chains, you could come to an agreement with a car dealer to offer key chains for free to all his customers. Of course, he has to pay for your key chains whenever he sells cars (this is different from buying a number of key chains from you at the outset which he may not agree with; he only pays you when he sells the cars).

Make it work for you!

> A property developer who finds it challenging to sell his newly built units offers to add furniture to the living room and the main bedroom as part of the deal. His offer becomes more appealing for people looking to purchase a house who don't have suitable furniture (the cost of the furniture is obviously factored into the real estate price by the developer). They see the house with the furniture and this means less hassle for them.

This Strategy puts this developer ahead of his Competitors, while the furniture shop gets the orders without having to do anything. Of course, the furniture seller will offer his products at a discounted price to the developer, but he has zero Marketing and Sales costs for those Sales.

A car is another example of Attractive Premium that can be added to the sale of the house. Some people may be happy or able to get a loan for buying a house, but they may not be willing or able to get one for purchasing a car, in which case a house that comes with a car will be an appealing option.

Happy Meal by McDonalds

TAKE ACTION NOW!

Write down 3 of your own products that could be used as Attractive Premiums, and why. Mention who will incorporate your products into their offering:

1. _____
_____
_____

2. _____
_____
_____

3. _____
_____
_____

Tactic #20

Encourage On-the-Spot Purchase via Urgency

Sell as if today is Black Friday. As if tomorrow is also Black Friday. And the day after...

Generate a sense of Urgency to encourage your **prospects** to purchase on the spot. Create scarcity around your product or offering: develop a **Limited Edition**, or a **Limited Stock**, or just a Limited Offer (a discount that is available for a short period only, even on a long-standing product of yours) and you will see increased Sales. Black Friday is one of the greatest inventions to facilitate On-the-Spot Purchases. Shops create a sense of Urgency by offering discounts on that day only. So you, the customer, either buy then and there at a discount, or you buy in the future and pay full price.

Of course, if today is Black Friday for one product, then the next Black Friday cannot be for the same product. Black Friday is never continuous, as it will then undermine the very effect it tries to create: Urgency.

Don't do offers every day because they de-value your brand!

People *consider buying* something to satisfy a Need, but *decide to buy* for very different reasons. One reason customers will buy on the spot is to ensure they get the product before stock runs out. And if stock is not likely to run out, then the offer (discount) should be limited (in time or on the number of products). Doing this influences people to make a purchase they might otherwise have postponed (perhaps forever). **Urgency is one of the most important characteristics of a successful business.**

Urgency helps you sell significantly more than you would otherwise

Why do you buy more when you go on holiday? Because you are not likely to ever go back to that shop, so the choice is between getting it now... or never. Create the same Urgency for your products and you increase Sales.

In 2013, I attended the National Achievers Congress in Amsterdam with a group of friends. The idea of this event is to provide great content for attendees, but also for the speakers to sell their products – usually further training and development programs – on the spot to a large audience. Often the speakers / sellers create a sense of Urgency by offering something for free to the first batch of customers or creating a rush to be 'accepted' into the program due to limited spaces. One of my friends noticed Robert Kiyosaki's 'Cash Flow' board game and wanted to buy it immediately. I suggested he wait to see if Kiyosaki offered a discount the following day, when he was due to appear on stage. My friend was adamant: 'No, I want to buy it now to be sure I get it. Have you seen how people rush to buy a product when a speaker is on stage? There are only a few games available and I don't want to miss my chance.'

Run to get the last product

Of course, the sellers display a small number precisely to create Urgency for purchase. They want the audience to buy now to avoid disappointment if stock runs out. However, stock is unlikely to run out. These are 'professional sellers' and they estimate the demand at such events and stock appropriately. They want to sell the maximum volume possible and this is just one of various techniques to encourage purchase on the spot.

Now we're talking!

> *Traditionally Nokia had always sold black phones – until they launched a **Limited Edition** of the same phone, but in pink. It was the first pink phone ever and was sold out within days due to its novelty and the scarcity they had created around it. I know because I got one! I paid a premium for it, but I didn't mind because I had managed to get my hands on something that others hadn't!*

Think how many coupons, vouchers or discounts you receive that are valid for 24 hours, or a week, or 'while stocks last'! See what they're doing?

Urgency not manufactured but engineered!

> *I recently went to a Nespresso shop on Regent Street in London to buy some more capsules. Note, I could order online, but I like the shop and the experience in the shop so much, that I prefer to go inside and feel the products before I choose them, and also look at the new stuff they periodically come up with.*
>
> *Every time I go, there is a limited edition of some cool-name coffee. This time it was Barista. Furthermore, within Barista, there is this special coffee, Ethiopia Yirgacheffe, which costs almost twice as much as a regular assortment, and sells better. Simply because one can only buy it now, while stocks last. They simply produce this limited edition as a "strategic product" that sells faster and for more money.*

Could they produce more of this coffee? I guess they could. But they don't on purpose. So they get suckers like us to visit their store to see what is new and pay more for their limited edition products.

Note, they present it with a story, because it is in fact due to the story that they can command higher prices. See Tactic #74 Use Core Stories, Volume 6.

ETHIOPIA YIRGACHEFFE

After years of patient searching and sampling, this coffee jumped off the cupping table and brought back to life the elusive and historical notes thought by many to have slipped away forever. This cup captures all the region's exquisite finesse: its typical white floral notes, brushed with hints of aromatic orange blossom and nuts.

AROMATIC FAMILY: FLORAL
AROMATIC PROFILE: WHITE FLORAL

COLOMBIA AGUADAS

The particular microclimate high up in the Aguadas region of Colombia, meant one pocket of farmers made their coffee in an unusual way, resulting in an extraordinary cup. Complex and with fine acidity this light-roasted espresso is particularly sweet, reminiscent of candied apples and red berries.

AROMATIC FAMILY: FRUITY
AROMATIC PROFILE: SWEET AND CARAMELIZED

TAKE ACTION NOW!

Write down 3 ideas for creating Urgency around your products / offerings:

1. _____
   _____
   _____

2. _____
   _____
   _____

3. _____
   _____
   _____

Tactic #21

Grow Your Sales

Encourage On-the-Spot Purchase via Better Offer

> *Add to your offering such that your offering becomes the obvious best choice even for undecided prospects*

Another reason customers buy on the spot is to *get more for the same price*. This presents another opportunity for you to increase your On-the-Spot Sales: offer a larger quantity for the same price, or a package that can be purchased for a better price than buying the products individually. This is another type of **Limited Offer** that induces a quick purchase decision.

They walk the talk!

Before deciding to invest in Infusionsoft, software that helps manage contacts and communication, allows for automated personalised campaigns, and more, I addressed an enquiry to the company. An Infusionsoft representative showed me how their software could help my business and I was clearly interested. I asked him to give me his best offer. His reply was $246 per month (instead of $299). When I said I would buy after the holidays (my original intention), he asked me to wait and put me on hold. Within a minute he came back to me with a proposal of $216 per month, including some additional benefits. The offer was valid only on that day. So I made the purchase. They had made me an offer that I could not refuse, both by decreasing the price and adding more to the product, to create a sale on the spot.

Note: If you consider using Infusionsoft, get in touch with us, because we have a working relationship with them and we can get you better prices.

Grow Your Sales

Get inspiration from your daily life

Think about your household shopping: you go to the supermarket to buy fresh bread and vegetables, and you end up also buying washing up liquid. It is a good deal: they offer a larger bottle of Fairy, with 50% more, for the regular price. So you buy the washing up liquid now, even though you just purchased some the week before and did not need any at that time...

TAKE ACTION NOW!

Write down 3 ideas for Better Offers on your existing products / services:

1. _____
   _____
   _____

2. _____
   _____
   _____

3. _____
   _____
   _____

Tactic #22

Know Your Customers. What Keeps Them Awake at Night?

> *Learn about your prospect's Challenges so you are relevant to their current Needs*

Know precisely the top five issues your clients are facing. Make it your business to know the kind of information they are interested in receiving. Ensure your salespeople know the areas in which your clients would like to see improvements in their businesses or lives. Become familiar with your clients' criteria for making a decision about buying a product like yours. Make sure the information you provide is relevant, that it addresses your clients' Interests and Challenges.

Your salespeople should also know the answers to the following:

- What do I really want to accomplish in this account or discussion?
- Why are some Prospects not buying from me?

Only by knowing what your Prospects need are you able to satisfy them. If you don't know what they really want, how can your offer be relevant to them? The more relevant you are, the more attracted your prospects become to your business.

My clients are business owners who want to attain more customers, more money, and more time for themselves – which is why I have structured this book as I have. Each tactic addresses a Challenge that a business owner may have. My Objective with this book is to help business owners reach their Goals. I do so by providing information relevant to their Challenges. This book is a bonus – by offering it for free to my clients and selected Prospects, I give them more than what they ask for. By providing them with what they need, I also create a Relationship with my prospects and clients, which makes them more likely to buy from me. The information I provide here is *relevant* to my clients. If it triggers more questions and they want to know more about how to apply these techniques to their businesses, they will buy more services from my business.

By being relevant to your customers, they listen to you and are interested in what you say – via emails, newsletters and billboards, and on your website. Why do you think online bounce rates are so high? Because visitors don't find the message relevant to them and they don't want to waste their time.

Here's why you need to do this!

> *A man enters a women's department store. The shop assistant asks, 'Are you looking for something special?' She starts a discussion in order to understand what the man wants so that she can show him relevant articles. Imagine if she had suggested lovely lingerie for his girlfriend, only to discover he was celebrating his mom's 80th birthday.*

> *Don't guess your clients' needs! Ask them!*

TAKE ACTION NOW!

Write down 3 Challenges that your customers are facing right now:

1. _____
_____
_____

2. _____
_____
_____

3. _____
_____
_____

Tactic #23

Grow Your Sales

Keep Close to Your Customers

> *Become your customers' friend and they will become your fan*

Build your Database with information about your customers and use it to maintain contact with them on a regular basis. If you are a retailer, collect basic information such as name and contact details. If you know their address, can you deduct their status, their spending power or the type of products they buy? (If you can't just yet, collect the addresses nonetheless and you will figure it out later.) Don't forget to collect email addresses to feed into your **Email Marketing** campaigns. Date of birth is important too – you might want to send a happy birthday voucher to show you care for them and to get them into your shop, spa, or business. Collect information about the products they buy, how often, and how much they spend in your shop. Use all this data to get closer to your customers. Inform them of products, special offers and promotions they may be interested in.

If you are a **B2B** company, your job is more difficult as you have to know all of the above for each contact person. You need to keep track of the people you deal with when they change jobs. Make sure you get introduced to the successor and that you know where your contact person has moved.

> *The more you know about your clients, the easier it is to sell to them*

The more one-to-one discussions involved in the Sales process, the more crucial this information becomes. Think of your company's top 20% clients. Each company has a contact person. For each contact person, your sales people should know things like: what will make them more successful as individuals, their ultimate Goal(s) in life, their hobbies, the number of children they have (and their ages and names). Basically, the sales representative has to become friends with his clients. Get to the point where you pay each other visits at home and outside of work.

The closer you get to your customers, the more often they come to you for purchase. People do business with people they like. People are more likely to buy from a friend than from a stranger. Become friends with your customers and Potentials and you have a better chance of selling to them.

> *Nobody wants to be sold to, but everybody wants to choose to buy.*
> *So make them buy from you!*

The more you know about your customers, the more you can adjust your offerings, your Sales process and your approach to be relevant to them. Being relevant adds Value to their lives and increases their interest in your business. They come to you for purchase when they need the product you sell.

I naturally become friends with the clients I like. As a result, whenever they have a business problem they come to me for a Solution, which means another consulting contract for my company. Alternatively, if I have a Solution that I know is a good fit for certain clients, I tell them about it and there is always a good chance they will buy it.

Put it into practice!

In essence, we are all retail clients. Have you ever received an email from a retailer and bought something you weren't really looking for... because it was there, just a few clicks away. (Or perhaps you were looking for the product but hadn't started your search for it yet.) The company that sold you the product was closer to you than their Competitors, and they made the sale. Maybe you wouldn't have purchased the product at all, or maybe you would have bought from another retailer... You bought it based on proximity.

TAKE ACTION NOW!

Write down 3 ideas on how to get closer to your customers:

1. _____
   _____
   _____

2. _____
   _____
   _____

3. _____
   _____
   _____

Tactic #24

Grow Your Sales

Contact All Customers Soon After Their Purchase

Start by simply saying 'Congratulations for your purchase'

You want to Stay in Touch with customers to show you care, though the aim is also to make another sale or to get another order in the future. Contact all customers within 10 to 20 days of their initial purchase. Do this via an email, a telephone call, or a letter – whichever you are more comfortable with. You can contact them to check their level of satisfaction, to offer another product or a discount, or to inform them of new products or of the benefits of their purchase.

Keeping in Touch with your customer post purchase can be as basic as saying 'thank you'. Courtesy has multiple benefits: it nurtures the Relationship, increases brand awareness, and (ultimately) paves the way for another sale or order. By Keeping in Contact, you also remind them you exist. When they need your product again, it's you they will think of.

Once I have signed a contract with a new client, I assign him a project manager. I know my consultants do an excellent job, but I nonetheless make a courtesy call. I do this to make them feel special and to show I care. Sometimes I receive Feedback that helps me improve my services, so I get double the benefit from these calls.

If you have so many customers that you can't possibly call them all yourself, either assign a person to call on your behalf or send an email.

Make it work for you!

> For a retailer, the job of following up with customers post purchase is simple. Amazon sends regular emails with relevant products based on your previous purchases. eBay sends offers to list your items for free as well as relevant products. Photo management site Shutterfly sends potential photo books (automatically designed) based on albums customers have created or offers on personalized items, such as a mug with the customer's photo. They also send special offers depending on prior purchases or lack of purchase and they always have special deals for Mother's Day, Christmas and other holidays.

TAKE ACTION NOW!

Write down 3 messages you would like to send to your customers post purchase, as well as the preferred means of communication (email, telephone, letter, postcard, etc.):

1. _____
   _____
   _____

2. _____
   _____
   _____

3. _____
   _____
   _____

Tactic #25

Grow Your Sales

Develop Partnerships

Join forces with a complementary business to get bigger bang for your marketing buck

There are various types of Partnerships that you can develop to increase Sales. We already saw the potential of marketing to your partners' customers (see Tactic #13) and the benefits of Association. One rule applies to all Partnerships: create a *win-win Relationship*. **Both parties must benefit from the Partnership.**

Such Partnerships help generate quicker and / or larger volumes of Sales. The effort of attracting customers is either shared between parties, or undertaken by one partner (in which case the 'passive' partner can sell more with no extra effort). If, for example, you have a large Database of customers, you can sell your partner's services to your customers and receive commission. Either way, you increase Sales, with good profit margins.

Some examples of types of Partnerships to inspire you! Use and combine them as you like.

- *Affiliate Marketing* refers to a contract whereby one business reaches customers for the other business in return for a percentage of any successful Sales. Your partner has access to a large number of your customers within your target market and promotes your product for a percentage of the Sales you make from his list. This Partnership is common online, where the Affiliate partner can charge you either a percentage of the sale, or for every visitor that comes to your site from his website, newsletter or any other action he has undertaken to attract customers to you. **Affiliate Marketing** is a great way to reach your dream clients quicker (those clients you consider the best match for your business). For example, we sell small business growth services. So a good **Affiliate Marketing** partner for us would be the Small Business Association (SBA), who has a trusted relationship with many small businesses. A Partnership with the SBA could give us access to their members. We would pay the SBA 10% of all Sales generated from their members. Everybody would be happy: we would get more clients and the SBA would get more income. If you have a strong online presence – through your website, email contacts or social networks – and connect with other small business owners, joining the Tooliers® Affiliate Program could be a great way for you to generate extra revenue. Find more information at *www.tooliers.com/affiliates*. It is very important to not approach Affiliates from the very beginning. I know it is tempting because it doesn't cost you anything to get leads or even clients this way. But it costs you a missed opportunity if you do it too early. Most people who act as Affiliates expect some level of income. So you need to be able to tell them the kind of sales you make from every 100 or 1,000 or 10,000 people approached. It is tempting to make some assumptions. Some people who are close to you and trust you may use those numbers. The problem is that in most cases such numbers are not attainable from the very beginning and you may end up disappointing your partner. Even worse, if we

> *Approach Affiliates ONLY after you have a saleable product and a sales system in place.*

are talking about a professional Affiliate, you only have one shot. And if you don't deliver the sales they anticipate, they will never do business with you again. So better save your bullets for when you have your saleable product and your sales system in place. Because then everyone wins!

- **Joint Venture (JV)** is a business arrangement in which two or more parties agree to pool their Resources for the purpose of accomplishing a Specific Goal. This might be a new project, or simply to generate Sales for one or both parties. Our business could, for example, partner with Infusionsoft (the software company whose offer I could not refuse; see Tactic #21 'Encourage On-the-Spot Purchase via Better Offer'). We both sell to small businesses and our products are complementary. By creating a JV, we could combine our efforts to attract customers for both of our businesses.

Approach a potential partner by proposing something of value to THEM

- **Cross Selling** involves selling one's products together with another business's Complementary Products. For example, I could create a Cross-Selling Agreement whereby I offer our business growth services packaged with website diagnosis and improvement from Woorank.com. The latter is a service that we can't offer ourselves, but it is relevant to our target market, who are interested in improving their websites as part of working on attracting more customers.

- In a ***Host-Parasite Relationship***, one business enters into a venture with another business with the aim of exploiting (on an ongoing basis) something valuable that the other company has – for the benefit of *both* businesses. **Attractive Premium** (see Tactic #19 'Turn One of Your Products into "Attractive Premium"') is an example of a **Host-Parasite Relationship**. The premium provider relies entirely on its partner to generate the Sales.

TAKE ACTION NOW!

Write down 3 types of business with which you could create a Cross-Selling Partnership. Briefly write the potential benefits to both parties:

1. _____
_____
_____

2. _____
_____
_____

3. _____
_____
_____

Identify 3 types of business with which you could create a Host-Parasite Relationship. Briefly write the potential benefits to both parties:

1. _____
_____
_____

2. _____
_____
_____

3. _____
_____
_____

Tactic #26

Grow Your Sales

Start a Relationship with Your Prospect

Offer something for free or at a low price to start a Relationship with your potential customer

Not everyone is ready to buy right away. They may not need your product or service, or they may not trust your brand (yet). This is why you want to start building Relationships with as many potential customers as possible. Some people appreciate your information about your product or service, but others may require a taste before buying it.

Offer a free trial, or a sample of what you do. Provide Value to your prospect before you charge anything. **People like to receive free stuff, and if they have had a good experience with your brand, they are highly likely to purchase from you.**

Think of your shopping at your local supermarket... did you get to taste yoghurt, a piece of ham or a cereal? Large brands do promotions like this all the time. They want you to taste their product (for free) and usually combine this with an On-the-Spot Promotion (see Tactics #17, #20 and #21 for strategies that create On-the-Spot Purchase). The idea is that once you have tried the product – and assuming you like it – they will then give you an even better reason to immediately purchase it, either by providing more quantity for the same price or a discount. Their main aim is to get you to consume their product in the hopes that you will become a regular customer.

They're already doing it!

Most SaaS (Software as a Service) companies use this tactic successfully. They let you use their software for a month for free, or they let you use a light version of their software free of charge, with the expectation that once you know the product and like it, you will become a paying customer for its additional features. Mailchimp offers a free emailing service if you have less than

2,000 users. But when your email list grows beyond this, you have to move to a paid solution, whereby they charge you $75 (or more) a month. If you like their free service, you are likely to upgrade and pay them to send more emails to more people. Your cost of starting a Relationship with them is zero, but if you later want to move, you have a bit of work to do, so it is usually easier to stay with Mailchimp and pay for the premium product.

This tactic works well for membership sites too, where your first month, or first post, or first listing is free. I search for tenants for my flat in London via www.openrent.co.uk. The first ad is free for five days. If you are lucky enough to find a tenant in five days, you don't pay anything. After this period, your ad will remain online, but not on the main property search sites; i.e. your chances of finding a tenant are close to zero. Having experienced and enjoyed the services of www.openrent.co.uk for free, I paid to have my ad published beyond the first five days. Offering those free days had hooked me in and enabled them to start a Relationship with me. I like the service so much that I will continue to use it whenever I need tenants for my flat.

One of the key strategies to be successful with online marketing is to offer the so-called Lead Magnet. This is usually a pdf report with useful information for potential clients, and for which people are prepared to "pay" with their email address.

This is how we use this strategy:

1. We place an advert to promote a webinar (of course one that has good content and is of value to our potential clients).

2. The webinar itself is a Lead Magnet (people must insert their email address to register).

3. The next page, right after the registration page, is the so called 'thank you page', which we use to get the person closer to buying from us.

The picture below shows the three steps. Please use these three steps rather as a principle than literally. Because, if you really want this to generate leads and sales for you, there are more interactions you need to set up around these three main steps.

In conclusion, when you give something for free, people are more willing to pay attention and it is easier to engage with them. In addition, some of the takers of the free offer will also take your paid offer.

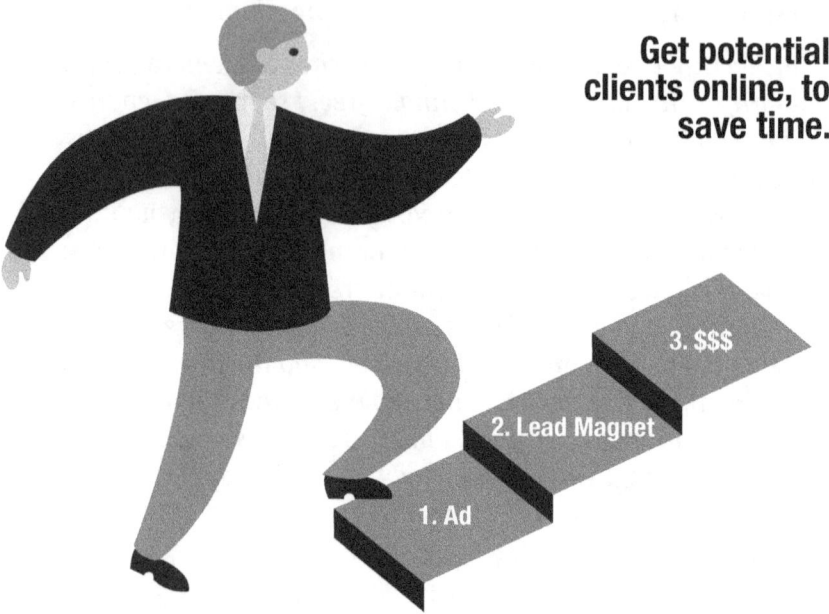

Get potential clients online, to save time.

TAKE ACTION NOW!

Write down 3 potential products or services you could offer for free (i.e. as a sample) to build a Relationship with potential customers:

1. _____
   _____
   _____

2. _____
   _____
   _____

3. _____
   _____
   _____

Tactic #27

Upgrade to a Sales Machine Organization

Constantly improve your Sales System

Great Sales are a matter of both personal talent and good organization. While the first is up to your Sales staff and can be managed only indirectly by you, the business owner, the latter can be methodically improved by following certain simple steps.

The internal organization of your Sales function can have a make or break effect. **Improve your internal organization** by following these basic rules:

1. Have a procedure to approach and deal with Prospects
2. Have weekly meetings for your Sales team
   a. Ensure your salespeople improve themselves in the weekly meetings, by sharing information, by observing what does and doesn't work and by learning from each other
   b. Review your Sales process constantly in the weekly meetings, with the aim of improving it
3. Analyze Customer Feedback and constantly improve your processes
4. Ensure you have a Reporting System that functions
5. Allocate the most difficult Sales to your Best Performers
6. Recruit and retain only the best
7. Remunerate your Sales team based on performance
8. Have administrative tasks performed by admin people and allow your Sales team to sell 100% of the time
9. Personally train the salespeople and ensure they exhibit the values you want them to have

Your salespeople should follow the seven steps of the selling process:

1. **Establish a rapport** with the Prospect. Your salespeople should spend 60% of their time on this. For example, see Tactic #22 'Know Your Customers. What Keeps Them Awake at Night?'
2. **Find Need.** For example, see Tactic #15 'Become the Confidant of Current and Potential Customers'.
3. **Build Value** around your company's offering. For example, see Tactic #11 'Tell Stories to Sell'.
4. **Create desire.** For example, see Tactic #26 'Start a Relationship with Your Prospect'.
5. **Overcome objections.** For example, see Tactic #17 'Use *Inducements* to Close Sales Now'.
6. **Close the sale.** For example, see Tactic #20 'Encourage On-the-Spot Purchase via Urgency'.
7. **Follow-up.** For example, see Tactic #24 'Contact All Customers Soon after Their Purchase'.

Ensure your salespeople are trusted and perceived as credible and Experts. Make sure they build Brand Loyalty, pre-empt Competitors, generate referrals and motivate action immediately. Your salespeople are the engine of your organization. Their performance reflects directly on the results of the entire company.

> *Chaotic sales processes lead to under-performing businesses*

TAKE ACTION NOW!

Write down 5 additional characteristics you would like your Sales System to have:

1. _____
   _____
   _____

2. _____
   _____
   _____

3. _____
   _____
   _____

4. _____
   _____
   _____

5. _____
   _____
   _____

Write down the next 5 actions you will undertake to put a Sales System in place, or to improve your existing System:

1. _____
_____
_____

2. _____
_____
_____

3. _____
_____
_____

4. _____
_____
_____

5. _____
_____
_____

Tactic #28 — Grow Your Sales

Position Your Product or Service Exclusively

*Stop chasing customers.
Make them chase you and your product or service*

This is my favorite Strategy. Although it is difficult to achieve, it is definitely worth the effort. In the ideal scenario your offering is so great that your target customers are clear they want it. It is so difficult to get, though, that your potential customers want it even more. Your potential customers have to 'qualify' to be able to buy this offering. This is where you need to get to.

The more Exclusive the product, the more desired it is – and the more willing people are to pay a premium for it. You don't have to sell Louis Vuitton bags or Jimmy Choo shoes to get there. Create this kind of Brand in your own industry. Why do people pay so much for a bag or a pair of shoes? Because of the quality, the design, the style, the Brand, the status associated with them... What is so special about these products apart from the aforementioned factors? *Not everyone can have them*. Exclusivity makes them even more special.

If you sell an online product, make it accessible by invite only. Get inspiration from www.asmallworld.net, a social site that offers Exclusive Deals and Events to members.

Even a regular product can have some extraordinary features that make it unique and can be played upon for marketing purposes. Annabel's is a club in London where you can be accepted as a member only if you get two recommendations from existing members. You can become a member only after a screening process that takes a year or more. This makes it a hugely desirable place, especially for those people who go out in London a lot and want to visit exclusive, high society values.

Even if your product doesn't have particularly unique characteristics, brand it via Association. Look at Nespresso: it is associated with George Clooney.

Grow Your Sales

Learn from the best!

Did you know that Hermes sells certain lines of bags for tens of thousands of dollars, and that you may have to wait months to be able to buy one? Why do you think the Hermes bags are so expensive and in demand? Because there is a limited number of them. Of course, Hermes could open up a new production line to satisfy all that demand – but that is not their Strategy. You have to 'qualify' before you are able to place an order. (Anyone who wants a Hermes bag needs to first have spent a minimum of $50,000 on other purchases.) Hermes' salespeople call this 'building a relationship with Hermes', which translates as spending loads of money in a Hermes shop before you can have a bag. Hermes 'uses' their bags to sell large volumes of other (super-expensive) products they have in store.

Business Unlimited

As you might have already guessed, I am a huge fan of Tony Robbins! He too uses the tactic of creating Exclusivity to sell at a premium. He offers a number of excellent products to business owners, but one needs to 'apply' or 'qualify' to be able to buy these (expensive) products; i.e. Robbins 'selects' you to spend money on his products. You are then more likely to purchase because you feel special and have 'qualified' for the Exclusive Products. And of course, now that you are finally permitted to purchase, you don't want to miss out. You might pay a premium for the product but you are happy to do so.

There is one essential condition to the success of this technique: you, like Robbins, have to be able to deliver both quality and great Value for money.

Pssst!

I model Tony's technique with my *Ozana's Inner Circle*™. This is a club where I closely work together with other driven entrepreneurs, and the only way to join the club is by participating in one of my bootcamps. I only occasionally accept members straight into the club, after careful consideration – so in other words they need to apply and provide extensive information about themselves and their business to be considered. I do this because I want to ensure every member fits in. This is because we work closely together and I personally hold myself responsible for their business growth. So I need to be comfortable that they have the willingness and the means to do the work, so they achieve smarter profits faster. And most importantly, I need to be satisfied that their attitude towards business and working with a mentor is the right one. Otherwise, they will not get the results, and would therefore be better off not joining my Inner Circle.

Make sure people understand why your offer is exclusive

TAKE ACTION NOW!

Write down 3 ideas you could apply in your business to position yourself as Exclusive:

1. _____
_____
_____

2. _____
_____
_____

3. _____
_____
_____

Tactic #29

Grow Your Sales

Follow Your Customer's Needs

Stay in the game. Constantly adapt your offering to the shifting Needs of your customers

The world changes faster than we realize, and so do the Needs of your customer. Make sure you know the Needs of your customer today (see Tactic #22 'Know Your Customers. What Keeps Them Awake at Night?'), and also anticipate your customer's Needs in the near future and in the long term. Study the market and the trends, the habits and the changes in your industry and constantly adapt your product and your offering. Ensure your offering fits the current market and be ready to adapt it to meet future demands.

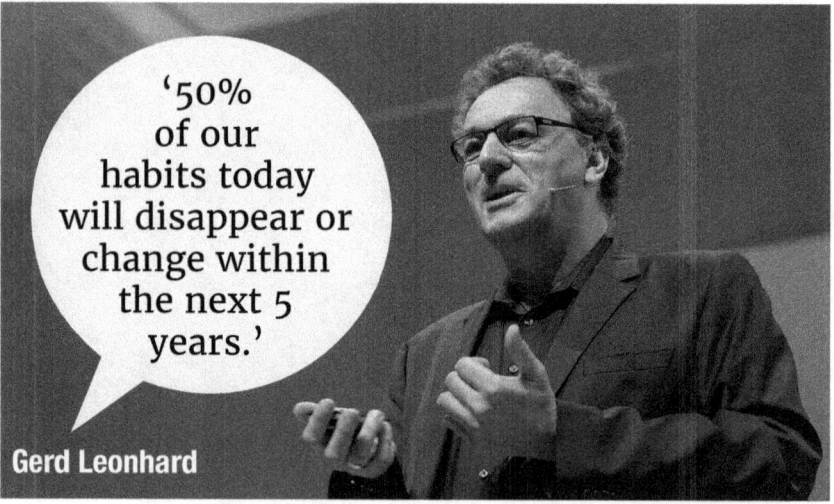

'50% of our habits today will disappear or change within the next 5 years.'

Gerd Leonhard

Refer back to Tactic #2: Developing Persona, the portrait of your ideal client. If you are not sure how to go about building Persona, particularly how to identify the real needs of your ideal clients, follow our Fast Track Implementation Plan to Developing Persona.

It gives you all the steps you need to take and answers all your most important questions, so you don't have to reinvent the wheel. Simply follow the process we have laid for you and get the right Persona for your business. You can find it at ***www.ozanagiusca.com/action-plan/persona***.

The advantage of adapting your offering to match demand is obvious. Less obvious is the consequences of not adapting it to the future. We have all seen new companies grow to be large and successful, and we have all seen large and successful companies go bust. **New companies are changing the rules of the game and you need to ensure you are a player in the 'new game'.**

This is why you need to adapt!

The internet may be a threat to some companies, but it is an opportunity for many more. Kodak, previously a top photographic company, is almost unheard of today, while Shutterfly, which stores photos online and offers printing services, has succeeded largely due to the internet.

We have also seen the effect of the internet on traditional businesses like media, where the rise of online news has led to a decline in printed media. If you were a media company 10 years ago, you would have had to change your offering to be successful today. Now look ahead another 10 years. Do you want to get there and think: 'I wish I had seen this coming 10 years ago'?

Think of companies like Google, Groupon, Booking.com, Amazon and eBay. Big names today – yet none of these existed 30 years ago. If you are not convinced, look at your own Needs today. Are they the same as they were five years ago?

TAKE ACTION NOW!

Write down 3 Needs of your customers today:

1. _____
_____
_____

2. _____
_____
_____

3. _____
_____
_____

Write down 3 Possible Needs of your customers tomorrow (what you think your customers will need in future):

1. _____
_____
_____

2. _____
_____
_____

3. _____
_____
_____

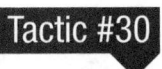

Grow Your Sales

Revisit Your Lists of Past Prospects and Customers

You already have a Relationship with a former customer. Exploit it to sell more

Take a look at all the customers and potential customers you have ever spoken to, enter them into a Database and revisit them. Call, email or make an appointment with the view to exploring new ways of collaboration – by which I mean making a sale (of course), but also creating possible Partnerships, where applicable. (See Tactic #25 'Develop Partnerships' for ideas on types of Partnerships.)

You already have a Relationship with these people. As you have had one or more interactions with them in the past, you are not cold calling them per se. **Assuming these customers had a positive experience with your company, they will be happy to receive your call**. You sold to them in the past, so why not sell again? If you don't do it, your Competitors will.

Make it work for you!

I used to offer assistance with fundraising to companies that wanted to take on an investment project or business owners who wanted to sell their companies.

In time, my business's Focus shifted towards helping business owners grow their companies organically, by attracting more customers and being more efficient internally, so they achieve smarter profits faster. When I wanted to grow my new business further, I emailed all previous clients and prospects with information on my new services. Twenty-four percent responded and requested more information – that was 100 or so hot leads for the new business. In addition, I received a number of lunch invites and the chance to catch up with old contacts face to face.

Business Unlimited

Email Marketing is still the best way to keep in touch with your prospective and existing clients, and to make more sales. You want to use Email Marketing because you want to stay close to your potential buyers, you want to be their first choice, so when they are ready to buy, they simply reply to an email and request your product or service... unless they don't buy via a click from your email. You also want to be there for people you've met once, perhaps in a networking event, who may need your product or service in a year. Such people are very unlikely to remember your name (or your company's name), hence your regular emails will remind them who you are.

Talking from my own experience, I remember I met a great designer few years back. At the time I could not afford his fees. But then, I got to a point where I could invest to get a fresh look for our business and I wanted to pay someone I knew was really good. I wanted to hire that guy right away... the problem was that I couldn't remember his name. Ironically, I had his contact details in my contacts on my computer and phone, but I didn't know who he was so couldn't find him. Had he sent me an email from time to time, I would have seen his name in my inbox and contacted him.

Can you see the importance of Email Marketing? It really helps your business significantly, provided you use it correctly. Because it is such a complex tactic and its success lies in details, I have prepared an Email Checklist for you – so when you next send an email to your clients or potential clients, you won't miss a thing. Grab your Email Checklist for free: **www.ozanagiusca. com/email-checklist**.

TAKE ACTION NOW!

Write down 5 actions you will undertake to start communicating with former customers:

1. _____
   _____
   _____

2. _____
   _____
   _____

3. _____
   _____
   _____

4. _____
   _____
   _____

5. _____
   _____
   _____

Tactic #31

Sell for Next Year, Not Just for Tomorrow

Though immediate Sales are important to the success of your business, remember to also focus your efforts on Long-Term Sales. By shifting from looking only short-term to looking long-term too, you ultimately create a situation in which you don't have to worry about tomorrow's sale. Wouldn't that be great?

Nurture your Leads and Potentials so they buy at some point, if it's not going to be now. Don't disregard them just because they are not potential customers today or in the near future. Look at the customer's Long-Term Value and not only at today's sale. **Develop a Long-Term Perspective for best results, because the value of one Long-Term Customer to your company is much greater than the initial sale**.

Open the tap towards the NEXT sale

At times this may mean you sacrifice big Profits today for Long-Term Business – for example by offering the first product for free or at a low price. (See Tactic #15 'Become the Confidant of Current and Potential Customers' and Tactic #26 'Start a Relationship with Your Prospect' for more information.)

Incentivize your customers to stay with you for the long haul

If you have a successful subscription-based product, I assume you offer great Value. Continue to do so and adjust to Future Needs (see Tactic #29 'Follow Your Customer's Needs') and your customers will stay with you long term. If you are not sure about the Value you offer to your customer, and people mainly buy your product on price, consider doing what many phone and internet companies do: offer a lower rate to your 'valued customers' to guarantee future Sales. Do you know what those phone and internet providers are really doing? They are giving you a discount (i.e. sacrificing profits now) in return for a two-year contract. We call this **Locking Sales In** for the future.

Provide credit towards your customer's next purchase

If you offer one-off products and subscriptions or contracts are not an option, you still need to give incentives for repeat business. An easy way to do this is to provide credit towards the customer's next purchase.

When I recently bought baby clothes from Osh Kosh B'gosh, the automated receipt included a 10% discount voucher – valid for a month, starting the next day – towards my next purchase. What the store did was to give me an incentive to come back within a month of my purchase. You might argue that once you've bought baby clothes, you will not need to come back. You are absolutely right. But you may suddenly consider buying a present for your friend's baby, or even giving her the 10% discount voucher.

Learn from the best!

> *My all-time favorite Tony Robbins masters all these techniques and more! When I bought his 18-month coaching program, it was automatically packaged with a $475 credit towards any Tony Robbins event I chose to attend in future.*
>
> *Robbins knows that I will have to pay more than that to attend another event, and he also knows that, by going to that event, I am more likely to buy further products from him. His offer of a credit is a way to nurture me and encourage me to stay with his company into the future.*

You don't have to run a multinational to use these strategies for locking in your Sales in advance. Understand the principles and tailor them to your own business.

TAKE ACTION NOW!

Write down 5 ideas to generate Long-Term Customers or Sales:

1. _____
_____
_____

2. _____
_____
_____

3. _____
_____
_____

4. _____
_____
_____

5. _____
_____
_____

Smart Business System™

In my experience, which includes being responsible for increasing the profits of 100 companies over the past three years – in some cases doubling and even tripling profits – I've noticed that most people running a small business or working alone, face 7 main challenges to increasing sales.

Many believe their lack of further success is due to legislation, taxation, red tape, banks not lending or the government not helping small businesses, but the truth is there are 7 challenges that are within your control to overcome, which makes all the difference.

It is important to understand these challenges, to identify which ones you are facing and then to use the very best system to overcome your specific challenges.

Because I also faced these challenges, specifically when I was struggling to sell with Tooliers *(www.tooliers.com)*, I have developed the **Smarter Business System™**, which is our battle-tested solution for achieving objectives faster.

My team and I have been using this system on a daily basis. Initially we kept it for ourselves and for a select group of clients. Now, we share it freely with fellow entrepreneurs, experts and driven professionals who want more.

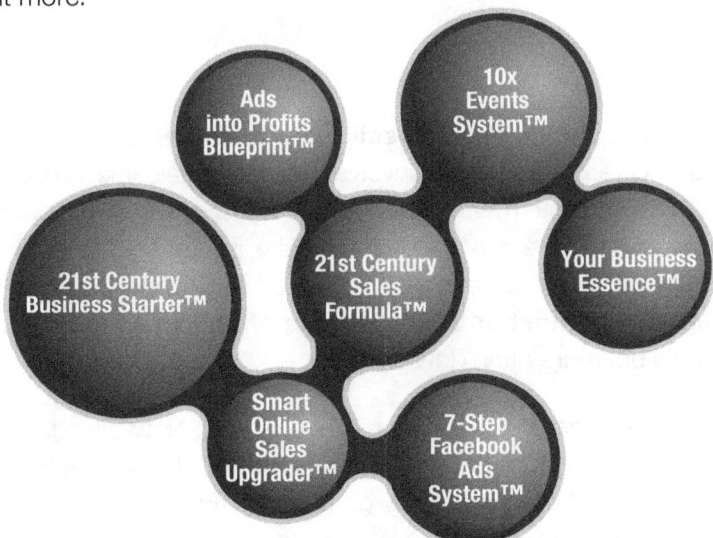

Smart Business System™

It is my pleasure to invite you to my online or live Master Classes in which I detail the system and its components.

Join me wherever it is convenient for you. Select from the events listed at **www.ozanagiusca.com/my-events** whatever best suits you and your needs. Some events are free and some require an investment.

Below I share more about the 7 challenges that block the growth of most businesses as well as the sub-system I have developed to overcome each challenge.

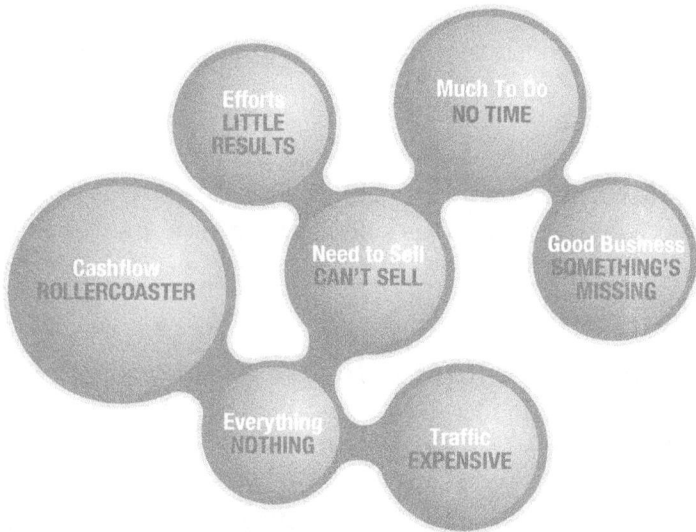

Challenge #1

Small business owners **want to sell more and have a stable, solid income**. Increasing the sales involves having a saleable product or service, a sales system and a way to feed this system with potential leads. Because there are various potential issues that need to be addressed before a business really takes off and grows exponentially, the **cash flow of most entrepreneurs is often like a rollercoaster** (sometimes up, more often down).

Too many meetings end up being a waste of time. Networking may be okay for social reasons, but few people buy from those they meet at events. A potential client suddenly goes cold... and whatever we do, it seems that people are simply no longer interested in buying.

Today, **people don't buy the way they used to**.

Due to the technology developments and the internet, the way people buy has changed. Which means that if you want to sell more, you also need to change your approach.

You need to adapt your business to the current reality. This is having the 21st Century Business Approach, the 21st Century Business Marketing Methods, and the 21st Century Business Essentials (this is not about the essentials in your business, which I am sure you have, but about the essentials that your business needs to give to you, its owner), because business as usual, as in the past, is no longer an option.

The key words here are Customer's Journey, a term that many experts talk about, but which is not understood and leveraged as it should be. This is about you **building a number of pre-programmed interactions with your potential clients, so you take them from "I don't know you" to buying from you and even recommending you to others**.

In most cases, such a 'journey' doesn't happen naturally. You need to engineer it, so your potential clients take the right steps (depending on where they are in relation to wanting your type of product or service) towards you and only you.

In order to build the road for such a journey, you need the 21st Century Business MAP.

21st Century Business MAP™

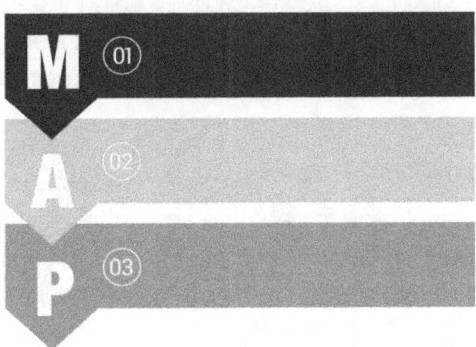

Smart Business System™

Deploying this system is the way to not only stay in business long term, but to thrive and generate increasing cash flow.

We are talking about combining online with offline activities, about talking to the potential client more but mainly in an automated or semi-automated manner, so you really leverage what you have and know so you achieve smarter profits faster.

I discuss this new approach and how to position your company, product or service and how to build your Customers' Journeys during the Smart Business Accelerator™ *(www.ozanagiusca.com/kim-en)*, strategic workshop over two days.

If you want to be in full control of your business; if you are fed up with trying various approaches which waste your money and time only to bring stress and frustration; and if you are committed now to investing to transform and scale your business, to maximize your profits and increase your impact so you achieve YOUR objectives, then I'm here to support you!

I invite you to join me for my next workshop where we will plan your Smarter Business *(www.ozanagiusca.com/kim-en)*.

Challenge #2

Before they started working with us, our clients were doing various activities, trying to sell to as many people as possible, but only getting a few clients.

I often see entrepreneurs busily developing a new product, serving existing clients, trying to source extra help, doing the admin tasks and even taking the trash out. They are constantly busy, feeling overwhelmed by how much they have to do… but what progress do they actually make?

For these entrepreneurs, I have developed the **Smart Online Sales Upgrader™**, to enable you to get more and better clients fast. Because generating business online can be done on auto or semi-auto pilot and when the system is deployed correctly, you have more time to do what you really love.

See in the illustration below how you can deploy this method to build your own system, to generate business online and have a constant and predictable cash flow.

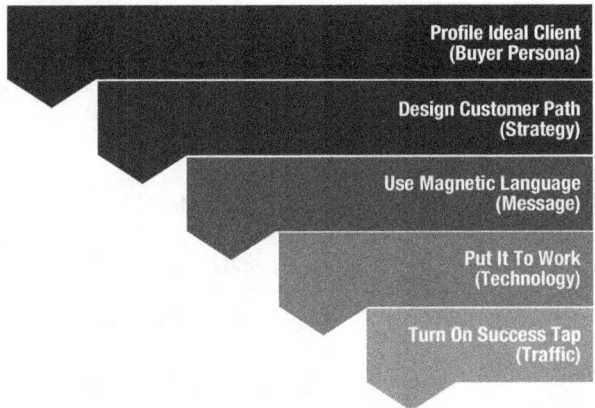

Under our guidance, participants in our Smart Online Sales Bootcamp™ *(www.ozanagiusca.com/sos-bootcamp-en)* achieve in two days what they have struggled to do on their own for years!

This method works because it has been tested on more than 400 entrepreneurs in most industries, ranging from professional services (consultants, coaches, experts) to manufacturing and retail.

The secret here is CLARITY. And to get clarity you need to go through a series of questions and, of course, answer them systematically, on paper.

Challenge #3

The majority of small businesses want more traffic in their store (online or offline) or visiting their website. Traffic is expensive, though, and they can't afford to waste resources on promotional activities that don't lead to sales.

We've figured that Facebook is the best platform right now to get traffic. It works for all businesses, but only when deployed correctly. If you are wondering if Facebook Ads are for you (i.e. investing in promotion on Facebook), join my next online Master Class *(www.ozanagiusca.com/facebook-ads-why-en)* on this subject.

Smart Business System™

We have developed the 7-Step Smart Business Facebook Ads System which we'll present during this Master Class. Simply go to **www.ozanagiusca.com/facebook-ads-system-en**, register, attend, take notes and implement.

We tested and tested… invested $100,000+ in our own campaigns and helped 300+ clients run profitable ads campaigns.

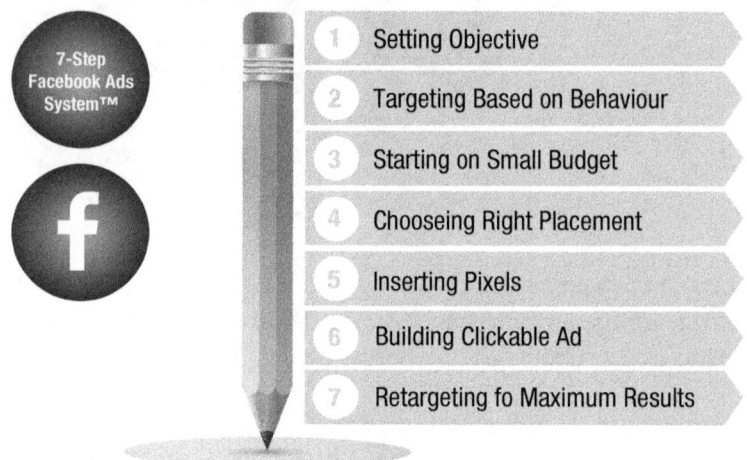

Challenge #4

Many people running their own show, be it a one-man venture or an established business, **need to sell but don't know how**. The truth is that selling is a skill you can learn. What's interesting is that most of our clients don't want to even consider taking sales courses. Because, just as they don't like others trying to sell to them, they know their potential clients don't want to hear from another pushy sales person. Besides, we set up our businesses based on our passion, because we want to help others and change the world, and we don't want to sound like second-hand car salesmen!

Many of my clients find themselves in a catch 22: they know their product or service is excellent but clients only realize and appreciate the value once they've experienced the product. Unable to clearly explain this amazing value to their potential clients, they have to constantly decrease their price just to make a sale.

The solution is the **21st Century Sales Formula™**, which is about helping your potential clients in advance so you show them, before asking for the sale, that you are the right person to help them.

The secret is to do it in such a way that you **create interest for your product or service so you don't even have to "sell" for a sale to happen**.

Imagine your best clients coming to you and begging you to sell to them!

Join my next Master Class on How to Accelerate Your Sales **(www.ozanagiusca.com/accelerate-sales)** to discover how easy this is. And yes, this is exactly what I do – I create interest and earn the trust of potential clients (like you) by offering real help in my Master Classes without any sales talk.

The more value you create in your marketplace, the more offers you can make. And of course, the more offers you make, the more sales you can achieve.

21st Century Sales Formula™

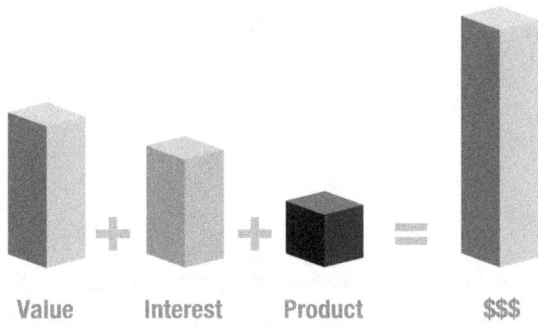

Value Interest Product $$$

Challenge #5

Most people in business have invested money, time and a lot of efforts in promotion, but the results are far from satisfying. This is because many tactics have been used in isolation without a strategy to back them up.

If you feel you have this challenge, then I highly encourage you to discover my Ads into Profit Blueprint™, where you can get answers to your burning questions about advertising, and more importantly, where you can ask more questions to help you get the RIGHT answers. Yes, it is only when you ask yourself the right questions that you can get helpful answers, so you can really get a good return on their promo budget.

Access Ads into Profits Master Class *(www.ozanagiusca.com/turn-ads-into-profitable-customers)* to get the right answers to the right questions.

Most entrepreneurs gain business in the traditional way. What you'll understand is how to expand beyond what you do well and break through the current sales figure, by adding other products, services, actions.

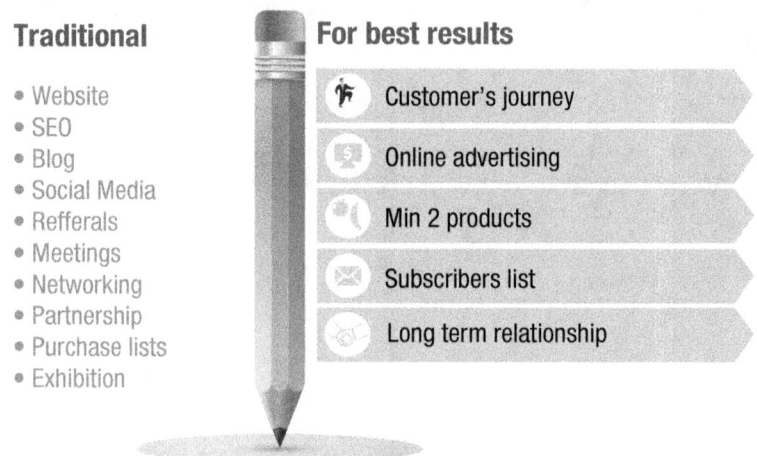

Traditional
- Website
- SEO
- Blog
- Social Media
- Refferals
- Meetings
- Networking
- Partnership
- Purchase lists
- Exhibition

For best results
- Customer's journey
- Online advertising
- Min 2 products
- Subscribers list
- Long term relationship

Challenge #6

Most people in business have a lot to do and not enough time to do it! They wish the working day had 48 hours so they could hold more meetings with potential clients and show their product to more people; to ultimately increase their sales and profits.

Well, there is a way for you to have 50 to 500 sales conversations in an hour or so. If you're asking yourself how this is possible, the **10x Events System™** *(www.ozanagiusca.com/10x-sales-bootcamp-en)* is for you.

Instead of giving away valuable information about your product or service during a sales conversation, share it in an educational or fun context, when your potential clients WANT to hear you talk about your offering.

The benefit of selling at events is that it is the most efficient way to sell, while getting your potential clients to love you for the experience and information you provide.

What do I mean by 'events'? It could be a workshop, a webinar, a series of online videos, a sampling / tasting or networking event, even a fashion show.

As you become closer to being an important player in your niche, you need to consider selling from the stage/ via events. This is not just for experts and trainers. Our clients who have introduced events in their marketing and selling activities include fashion, car repair, consultants, kids development, agricultural equipment, even doctors.

Of course, we are not talking about just any event! There is a way to hold events of the highest quality, which I share with you in the **10x Events System™** *(www.ozanagiusca.com/10x-sales-bootcamp-en)*.

Challenge #7

Whether an established business or a newcomer, we all want to make more money. For some, money is a means to living the desired lifestyle, and for others it's a means to show they've achieved a lot and gained the appreciation and respect they deserve.

The challenges are that due to daily activities, and fires that need to be put out, entrepreneurs forget about their destination and most often behave as if lost in a dark forest.

In addition, in a world with so many people trying to sell so much it is difficult to grab your clients' attention. In a world where it is hard to get the right employees, and where communication is so important... it is not easy to 'construct' the right messages that attract the right people. You need to formulate your messages, with a view to ensuring that they are short and to the point, but most importantly, that they get to the heart of your potential clients. Such communication depends on the clarity you have about yourself and your business, and the connection between the two.

Smart Business System™

Unless you have a set of key messages that you and your team consistently use, you are just another seller, talking in generic terms like most people. This means you are forced to keep your price to a minimum, rather than getting paid for the real value you provide.

In other words, you need to carefully draft your key messages to use as your introduction, as a conversation opener or even on stage when you speak in front of more people. In order to get it right, you need to go to the essence of your business.

This is YOUR job!

No external consultants can come up with your key messages because they have to represent you. And the good news is that when you work on identifying such messages, you'll reconnect with your business and fall in love with it all over again.

The outcome is the right foundation for your communication, and you'll really become unstoppable and truly fulfilled when you answer the 7 WHY-based questions shown in the illustration below.

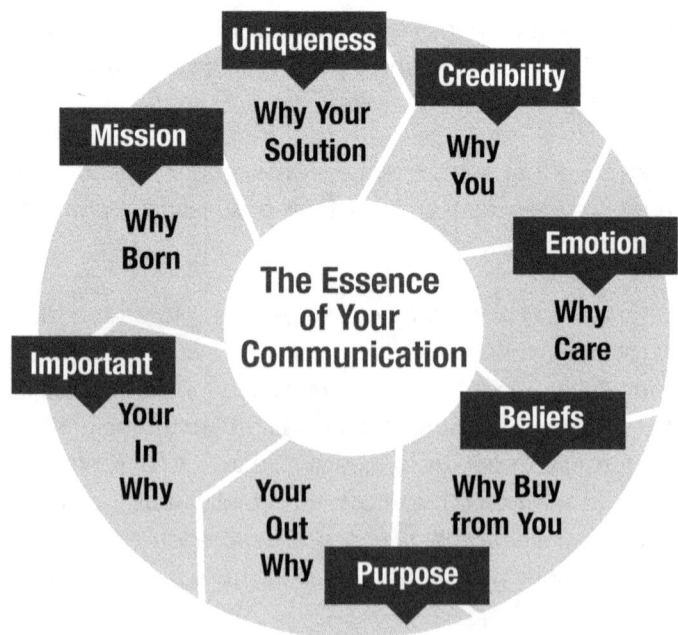

Big companies spent tens of thousands of dollars to identify their key messages. We've created a process to help you distill your key messages without spending an arm and a leg.

Would you like to overcome any of these challenges?

Then I invite you to join my **Smart Business Accelerator™** *(www.ozanagiusca.com/kim-en)* to discover how to build your Smarter Business, your business anchored in the current reality, and adapted to your current needs, aligned to your heart, so you feel in control and get to your destination faster.

Let's spend two days together, and you will

- Evaluate your growth opportunities to unleash the full potential of your business

- Eliminate time wasters, so you really focus on what is most important for you

Leave this workshop with clarity, ways to upgrade your business and a plan of action so you achieve your objectives faster.

Bonus: Love Letter

More value to you

I write about giving more Value than anticipated to your clients, about amazing your customers, about giving something for free. Here, it is my freebie to wow you.

Following, you will find the easieast way to come up with your marketing strategy. I give you the tool so you define your marketing strategy in 30 minutes. The tool is in the form of a letter you write to yourself as if it was written by your Best Customer. I call it 'Love Letter' because it shows the love your customers have to your company. It looks like a testimonial, but it is much more than that. Fill in the blanks. The point of this letter is to help you really understand your business, and what matters for your business's success. It looks like a testimonial, but it is way more than that. Once this letter sounds right, you know the recipe for your business's success. You have more clarity about your own business. You just need to execute correctly (You can do that by applying the 101 tactics in this book).

Below you will find a template for your Love Letter, as well as the letter I wrote for Tooliers®. This helps me 'name' my Persona, the benefits of my product (both logical and emotional), the impact my product has on customers' lives, how to find our customers, what to use to find customers, what I want my customers journey to be, how to ask them to provide recommendations, and more.

This template is your Strategy in a nutshell! And yes, you can use this to get inspiration for what you want your (real) client testimonials to look like.

I challenge you to fill in the blanks for your business. If you want the original, so you don't have to type up the template, visit **www.ozanagiusca.com/love-letter/** and grab your copy for free.

Love Letter Template

Dear **[Company Name]**,

My name is **[Persona's name]** and I must tell you I love your **[product type]** and I feel compelled to tell you my story.

I am a **[business type / life or lifestyle role]** who **[problem / passion statement]**. Thing is, that **[impact of pain / passion to life]**.

But **[Product Name]** changed my life.

Whenever I **[do specific things with product]** it works exactly as promised. Not only do I **[specific benefits]** but it makes me feel **[strong emotional reaction]**.

I find I use the product in that way every **[time period: hour / day / week, etc.]**

It's as if you looked me in the eye and said, '**[Persona's name]**, I promise you **[value promise]**'.

What I didn't expect, and share with other **[why shares with]** by **[mean of 'sharing']** is that you made me feel **[emotion impact]**.

Your product has forever **[how life changed]**.

I first heard of your product while **[activity / place related to title or life role]**. I decided to learn if it was really meant for me, so **[how to get more info]** where you said **[key message promise]**, which spoke directly to me. To tell you the truth, at first I was skeptical. But then, when you provided **[activity to induce trust]** I knew you were the right company.

[Influencer] endorsing the product was also key.

Still, I felt **[primary concern / objection]**.

Finally, when **[final action]** I was ready to **[sign up / buy / try]**.

I couldn't wait to get going, so as soon as I could, I **[first product setup / interaction]** to get started, and very quickly tried the **[feature to realize promise]** which made me feel hopeful that I had made the right decision.

Love Letter Example

Dear Tooliers®,

My name is Elisabeth. I must tell you that I love your Marketing Lens™ Diagnosis and Growth Program and I feel compelled to tell you my story.

I am an accounting firm owner who needs more clients. Thing is, I'm not earning enough. But Marketing Lens™ has changed my life.

Whenever I think of investing in marketing activities, I use the Marketing Lens™ and it works exactly as promised. Not only do I discover free ways to attract clients, but it also makes me feel like I really master marketing as a whole. I find myself working on one action to grow my business every other day, for only 15 minutes per day. I started this just one month ago and I already see 10% more enquiries from potential clients.

It's as if you looked me in the eye and said, 'Elisabeth I promise that you will discover ways of getting more customers by yourself without spending a cent.'

What I didn't expect, and I share this with other accounting firm owners in our regular ACCA meetings, is that you made me feel like a great businessperson, not just an accountant. I truly *feel* I own my business now; I am not just a simple accountant who has a job in my own company.

Marketing Lens™ Diagnosis and Growth Program has forever changed how I market our accounting services.

I first heard of your product while browsing The American Institute of CPAs online. I decided to learn if it was really meant for me and I went to www.tooliers.com. You said that I would get answers to questions I had never asked myself and this really resonated with me. To tell you the truth, at first I was skeptical about getting actions tailored to my business and given automatically to me by a computer! No one knows my industry better than me. But then, when you provided the Marketing Lens™ Diagnostic Report I knew you were the right company. Your assessment of why I was not attracting the customers I wanted was

Love Letter

spot on. You also showed me what I need to focus on attracting the customers I deserve.

Entrepreneur.com's endorsement of Marketing Lens™ Diagnosis and Growth Program was also key to my decision to check you out. They are a trusted resource with information for every business owner.

Still, even at this stage I felt marketing was too complicated for me. Besides, I truly love performing accounting services, *not* marketing my business. Finally, after having followed the Action Plan on Social Media, I was ready to buy the Marketing Lens™ Growth Program. I understand now that things are not as complicated as they seemed, and that even I can attract and engage online with potential clients for my firm!

I couldn't wait to get going, so as soon as I could, I performed the Marketing Lens™ Diagnosis. I quickly started with the first action on Sales Funnel Tactic, which made me feel comfortable that I'd made the right decision. I see how, by the end of the Growth Program, I will have become a marketing guru for my business; customers will come to us, as bees are attracted to a honeypot. And you know what? I now see myself as *managing an accounting practice*, and no longer as doing accounting services. The latter is the job of my employees!

Love Letter

> **Want to grow your business and don't know how and where to start?**

> **Or do you have a business challenge you want an expert opinion on?**

I love bringing new ideas to the table and contributing to the growth of any kind of business, from e-commerce sites to professional services providers; from retail to entertainment. Every industry has its own particularities, but all have one thing in common: **apply best business practices and your business will succeed.** It's exactly this subject that I've mastered, and I can help any business implement best practices, regardless of size, industry or geography.

So contact me via my website and I'll respond within 24 hours.

www.ozanagiusca.com

If you just want to stay in touch, connect with me on:

- www.facebook.com/giusca.ozana
- plus.google.com/+OzanaGiusca
- www.linkedin.com/in/ozanagiusca
- www.twitter.com/OzanaGiusca
- www.youtube.com/user/ozana197

Glossary of Terms

These definitions are crafted to be as simple as possible, and are explained in the context of this book.

AAA rating - refers to the evaluation of credit worthiness; i.e how trustworthy a company is to do business with. The highest rating is AAA, descending to C (low) and D (even worse).

Action Plan or Fast Track implementation Plan - a step-by-step guide to work on and improve various areas of the business (strategy, sales, marketing, etc.) and sub-areas (educational marketing, writing blogs, building a website, email marketing etc.).

Affiliate Marketing - this is an agreement whereby a business rewards someone (affiliate person or company) for each visitor / customer brought by the affiliate's own marketing efforts, or for each purchase generated by the affiliate, within a time frame.

Attractive Premium - an item included in a pack, together with less interesting items, and sold as a bundle. It's a good way of moving slow-selling products.

Automate / Automating / Automation - using software rather than employees to undertake automatically some processes within the company.

Business-to-business (B2B) - a business that sells to other businesses. Compare with Business-to-Consumer (B2C), which is when the company sells to consumers / individuals.

Better Offer - a product (service) or a bundle of products (services), designed to offer more value (than usual) for the same dollar spent.

Brand - the name, design, symbol, colors or any other feature that identifies one company or product. For example, Coca-Cola is one brand, Fanta is another; they both belong to The Coca-Cola Company.

Branding via Association - linking the brand of one business with a better known brand, so the lesser known brand 'borrows' from the popularity of the other.

Business Doctor - business growth solution consisting of (i) diagnosing a business (see Business Lens®), (ii) designing a customized action plan to optimize and grow the company and (iii) implementing that plan.

Business Lens® - company assessment toolkit to show business owners the naked truth about their company. It identifies unexploited growth potential. It covers everything that matters for the growth of the business (analyzes in detail 15 business dimensions, including Strategy, Innovation, Leadership, Superstar Organization, Marketing, Sales, Human Resources, Motivation, Support Systems, Follow-Up and Organizational Culture) a Tooliers® service.

Business Lens® Diagnostic - the process of answering multiple choice questions and getting a business evaluation report that shows what the business does well and what it needs to focus on a Tooliers® service.

Buying Criteria - the requirements and rules that one buyer uses to buy a product, such as quality, price, availability, reliability, durability, comfort, habit, safety, freshness, coolness, taste, production methods, etc.

Chunking - grouping together information into ideally sized pieces, so they can be used effectively to produce the outcome one wants without stress or shutdown.

Chunk Down - dealing with smaller parts of information / activities in order to understand or do them effectively. Especially useful when the information / activities are new or complex.

Chunk Up - dealing with larger parts of information / activities in order to understand / accomplish more at once. Especially useful when one faces known information or deals with routine activities

Complementary Product (Service) - product (service) whose use is interrelated with the use of another product (service); e.g. cartridges and printers are complementary products.

Cross Selling - one business selling its product (service) to another business's customers, and vice versa.

Distribution Channel - the path through which products travel from vendors to consumers; e.g. coffee travels from farmer to exporter, to importer, to distributor, and to the retailer who sells to the end user.

Educational Marketing - sharing valuable information with potential customers, for their benefit and to build trust.

Gift with Purchase - providing another product (service) when someone buys a certain product (service); e.g. a sample cream when you buy a perfume.

Host-Parasite Relationship - adding one's product to be sold passively together with another product that is marketed and sold by the other business (the 'parasite' company doesn't do anything to make sales happen). E.g. producer of a dress adds belt from another manufacturer, and promotes and sells the dress with the belt.

Inducement(s) - an incentive to make the offering more appealing to the customer, and the sale sweeter.

Joined Offers - offering one's product together with another product; both parties promote the combined offer.

Joint Venture (JV) - business agreement for a set period, in which each party undertakes some efforts, for the benefit of all parties.

Lead - term used for a potential customer in the first stage of a sales process; i.e. the business made the initial contact with that prospect, be it (directly or indirectly) via the business's website, or via a phone call or meeting.

Lead Nurturing Email - email designed to build relationships and trust with prospective customers in a consistent and relevant manner.

Limited Edition - the manufacturing of a product in a limited quantity, to make it a more interesting purchase for the buyer.

Limited Time Offer - an offer that has a specific deadline, to give potential buyers a clear reason to act without delay.

Limited Stock Offer - a limited number of items made available, to give potential buyers a clear reason to act without delay.

Locking Sales In - securing long-term sales; e.g. signing a long-term contract or ensuring customer comes back for repeat purchase.

Offer Email - an email to promote a product, to ask for a purchase.

Potentials or Prospects - potential customers.

Pre-emptive Anti-competition Strategy - a strategy employed by one business to lead potentials to only consider its offering, thus blocking its competitors even before they are considered by the buyer as potential sellers.

Risk Reversal - marketing strategy based on removing the risks of the buyer to help them make the purchase decision; e.g. 30-day money back guarantee.

ROI (Return on Investment) - a performance measure calculated as the benefit produced by an investment divided by the cost of that investment (expressed as %); commonly used to evaluate the efficiency of an investment or to compare different real or potential investments.

Glossary of Terms

ROTI (Return on Time Invested) - the return on the time invested into an activity or project (valued in dollar amount per hour).

Sales Funnel - a metaphoric description of the sales process from initial contact to final sale. It is called a 'funnel', because there are many leads (cold potentials), and as one gets closer to the sale, the number decreases.

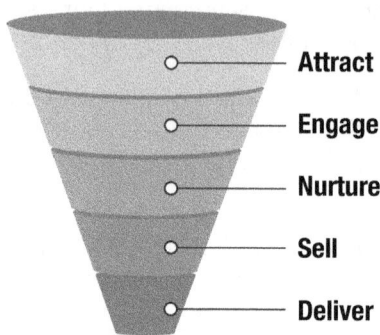

- Attract
- Engage
- Nurture
- Sell
- Deliver

Soft Skills - a cluster of personality traits, social abilities, communication, language, and personal habits that characterize relationships of one person with others.

Tooliers® - online platform with business growth tools designed to help small and mid-sized business owners to take their companies to the next level. Founded by Ozana Gusca.

Ultimate Strategic Position (USP) (not to be confused with Unique Selling Proposition) – the final perception that a company wants to have in the eyes of the customer.

Unique Value Proposition (UVP) - a few words used by one business to tell prospective customers why they should buy their product or use their service; it tells how this business adds more value or better solves a problem than competing businesses (similar to Unique Selling Proposition).

Value Papers - promotional materials (such as flyers, leaflets, brochures, catalogues) that give, besides the usual information / advertising content, monetary value to the holder towards the purchase of the product / service being promoted (such as % discount, $ reduction, gift); the goal is to incentivize a sale.

> 'Any ending is a new beginning.'
> Ozana Giusca

Make the most of the knowledge you have received or gotten from this book and take your business to the next level.

In this series

www.ozanagiusca.com/BusinessUnlimited

www.ingramcontent.com/pod-product-compliance
Lightning Source LLC
Chambersburg PA
CBHW070304230526
45470CB00002B/719